MORRISTON

D1327725

Tynnwyd yn ôl
SWANSEA LIBRARIES

6000284616

Withdrawn

Flavours of Wales

THE SEA SALT COOKBOOK

Gilli Davies and Huw Jones

GRAFFEG

The Sea Salt Cookbook
Published in Great Britain in 2016 by
Graffeg Limited

Text by Gilli Davies copyright © 2016.
Photographs by Huw Jones copyright © 2016.
Food styling by André Moore.
Designed and produced by Graffeg Limited
copyright © 2016

Graffeg Limited, 24 Stradey Park Business
Centre, Mwrwg Road, Llangennech, Llanelli,
Carmarthenshire SA14 8YP Wales UK
Tel 01554 824000 www.graffeg.com

Gilli Davies is hereby identified as the author of
this work in accordance with section 77 of the
Copyrights, Designs and Patents Act 1988.

A CIP Catalogue record for this book is
available from the British Library.

All rights reserved. No part of this publication
may be reproduced, stored in a retrieval system
or transmitted, in any form or by any means,
electronic, mechanical, photocopying, recording
or otherwise, without the prior permission of
the publishers.

ISBN 9781910862049

1 2 3 4 5 6 7 8 9

CONTENTS

Sea Salt

With over 750 miles of coastline, it is no surprise that Wales makes the best of its marine resources.

Coastal fishing, gathering seaweeds and collecting shellfish are all activities that have been with the Welsh for centuries and still continue today. The production of sea salt was also part of this Welsh coastal heritage until the late 18th century when the production team were fined for adulterating the sea brine with Cheshire rock salt and the business halted.

It was along the coast of Anglesey that this salt business had flourished due to the natural and swift flow of clean sea water through the Menai Straits. It was this natural abundance of all the right factors that brought Alison and David Lea-Wilson to consider re-introducing salt production at the site of their Sea Zoo in Brynsiencyn in 1999. It wasn't long before they had developed their own brand of Anglesey Sea Salt, also known in Welsh as Halen Môn.

Salt was once, before refrigeration, a much needed resource for preserving and curing meat and fish.

So valuable has salt been to man over the centuries, that at one time cakes of salt were used as money in Ethiopia and elsewhere in Africa and Tibet.

In the Roman army an allowance of salt was made to officers and men, and in imperial times, this salarium (from which the English word salary is derived) was converted into an allowance of money for salt.

Sea salt is made through the dehydration and crystallisation of seawater, and because the salt is obtained naturally from the sea, and does not go through any processing that alters the natural make-up of the salt, it contains many essential trace minerals that your body needs in order to be healthy. Naturally, the Welsh think their Anglesey sea salt is the best, and judging from worldwide sales, a lot of other people think so too! In fact, in 2014 Halen Môn was granted Protected Designation of Origin status by the European Commission.

The process at Brynsiencyn involves taking seawater, which has already passed through the natural filters of a mussel bed and a sandbank in the Menai Strait to be filtered through charcoal before being boiled at a low temperature. As the water releases steam it turns into a very salty brine which is turned into shallow crystallization tanks to allow the sea salt crystals to form. These are harvested by hand and the flakes are finally rinsed in brine until they shine.

If we are encouraged to eat less salt for our health, then let's make sure we eat the best. Salt brings out the flavour in our food and many people find that there is something quite outstandingly delicious about the soft flavour and crispy crunch of sea salt flakes .

Salty Tips
- Serve hard boiled quail's eggs with flakes of celery sea salt.

- Sprinkle potato wedges with sea salt before baking.

- Brush fresh asparagus with olive oil and sprinkle with sea salt before roasting.

- For great pork crackling, start with the best pork you can find and, if wrapped, allow the skin to dry out. Brush with sea salt and roast at a very high temperature until the crackling has set, then turn down to cook through.

- Add vanilla sea salt to chocolate or strawberries.

FOCACCIA

This recipe makes a tray of crunchy, tasty focaccia - perfect to quell the hunger of a crowd of friends on the beach, at a barbecue, or simply to pick at when peckish.

FOCACCIA

Ingredients

750g strong white flour

2 teaspoons salt

1 packet easy blend fast action dried yeast

2 tablespoons olive oil

¾ pint warm water

Olive oil, rosemary, chopped olives, halved cherry tomatoes and flakes of sea salt to sprinkle over the top

Serves 6-12

❶ Mix the flour with the yeast and salt.

❷ Pour in the warm water and oil and mix to a dough.

❸ Knead well for 5 minutes then spread the dough over an oiled baking tray.

❹ Leave to rise until doubled in size (about 1 hour).

❺ Make indentations with your finger across the dough and then dribble over the olive oil and scatter over sprigs of rosemary, chopped olives, halved cherry tomatoes and sea salt flakes.

❻ Bake in a hot oven (200°C) for about 20 minutes.

SEA SALT-MARINATED
SALMON WITH HONEY
AND MUSTARD SAUCE

This is the classic Scandinavian recipe of Gravad Lax, a clever sweet and sour mix which suits raw salmon so well.

SEA SALT-MARINATED SALMON WITH HONEY AND MUSTARD SAUCE

Ingredients

350g fresh salmon fillet

2 teaspoons sea salt

2 teaspoons caster sugar

1 tablespoon fresh dill, chopped

1 tablespoon parsley, chopped

Freshly ground white pepper

1 teaspoon grated lemon rind

For the sauce

3 tablespoons olive oil

1 teaspoon French mustard

1 teaspoon runny honey

1 teaspoon lemon juice

Seasoning to taste

Serves 4-6

1 Remove any bones from the salmon and lay the fillet down the centre of a piece of clingfilm. Scatter over the salt, sugar, dill, parsley, pepper and lemon rind. Wrap tightly and leave in the fridge for 24 hours.

2 For the sauce, simply combine all the ingredients in a screw-top jar and shake vigorously until well blended.

3 Serve the salmon, at room temperature, in thin slices cut down through the fillet.

4 Garnish with dill and serve the sauce separately.

LADY LLANOVER'S
SALT DUCK

An old fashioned recipe by Lady Llanover which emphasises how salt softens the flesh and draws out excess fat from the duck. Allow 3 days of preparation for this dish.

LADY LLANOVER'S SALT DUCK

Ingredients

1.75kg – 2.25kg duck

100g sea salt

2 medium onions, chopped

50ml water

1 level tablespoon plain flour

300ml milk

Serves 4-6

1 Rub the salt well into the flesh of the duck, turning and recoating every day for 3 days.

2 Keep the duck in a cool place throughout the salting process.

3 Thoroughly rinse the salt off the duck and place it into a large pan or casserole.

4 Pour over cold water to cover, bring to the boil and simmer very gently for 45 mins, turning over half way through. Then take the duck out and rest for 15 mins. Place the duck into a hot oven at 200°C for 15-20 mins or until the skin is golden brown and crispy.

5 Stew the chopped onion very, very gently in the water for about 15 minutes, until tender. It may be necessary to press some greaseproof paper down on top of the onions to retain the moisture.

6 Strain off the liquid and blend it with the flour, using a whisk.

7 Add the milk and then return the mixture to the onions.

8 Bring the onion sauce to the boil. Simmer for a minute or two in order to cook the flour and thicken the sauce.

9 Either liquidise or sieve the sauce, and taste for seasoning.

10 Serve the duck sliced with the sauce. A fruity chutney tastes great with this dish.

WHOLE SEA BASS
BAKED IN SEA SALT

A real party dish this, especially if you serve the sea bass at the table still in its salt coat then crack it off to reveal perfectly cooked and very moist flesh.

WHOLE SEA BASS BAKED IN SEA SALT

Ingredients

500-700g seabass, cleaned and scaled

Freshly ground black pepper

1 lemon, peel grated then sliced

2 tablespoons each of chopped thyme and rosemary

1kg coarse sea salt

1 egg white with 2 tablespoons water, lightly beaten

Olive oil

Serves 3-4

1 Heat the oven to 220°C.

2 Season the inside of the fish with pepper and add the slices of the lemon.

3 Mix the thyme and rosemary with the sea salt, lemon zest and beaten egg white.

4 Put $1/_3$ of the salt mix in a roasting tin with the fish on top. Completely cover the fish with the rest of the salt mix. Bake for 35-40 minutes.

5 To serve, crack open the salt case, remove the skin and head, then lift out the fish flesh, chunk by chunk.

6 Drizzle over olive oil before serving.

SPICED CHRISTMAS
LAMB

It's not traditional to serve lamb at Christmas but cold meat is always useful when feeding a crowd and this dish is delicious and unusual.

SPICED CHRISTMAS LAMB

Ingredients

1 breast of lamb, boned and excess fat cut out

Sprinkle:

2 teaspoons sea salt

1 teaspoon black pepper

Pinch of ground allspice and cloves

Rub:

1 tablespoon sea salt

1 dessertspoon of soft brown sugar and a good pinch of saltpetre (if available)

Serves 4

1 Sprinkle the breast of lamb with the sea salt, black pepper, allspice and cloves.

2 Roll up the lamb and tie or secure, then rub over the sea salt, brown sugar and saltpetre (potassium nitrate).

3 Turn the lamb and leave in the fridge for up to a week, recoating with the mix daily.

4 Rinse the lamb in cold water then simmer for at least one hour until it is soft when pierced.

5 Serve cold, sliced with sweet chutney

CHICKEN BAKE WITH SALTED PEANUT TOPPING

This nutty, crunchy topping brings a great flavour and texture to the chicken and the dish is quite simple to prepare.

CHICKEN BAKE WITH SALTED PEANUT TOPPING

Ingredients

4 chicken breasts, cut into large chunks

1 tablespoon olive oil

1 medium onion, sliced

1 tin chopped tomatoes

Sprig of fresh thyme

Good pinch of chilli flakes

1 glass white wine

Salt and pepper

Topping:

1 heaped tablespoon salted peanuts

1 clove garlic, crushed

Grated rind of one lemon

Serves 4

1 In a heavy-based casserole, heat the oil and fry the onion slices gently until soft. Add the chicken chunks and turn in the hot oil until they are coloured on all sides.

2 Add the chopped tomatoes, fresh thyme, chilli flakes, white wine and salt and pepper.

3 Bring to the boil, cover the casserole and cook gently either on the hob or in the oven for 20 minutes.

4 In the meantime, chop the peanuts with the garlic until they are about the size of couscous, then mix with the grated lemon peel.

5 Sprinkle over the topping just before serving.

ROAST PORK WITH
CRACKLING, SAGE, CIDER
AND CARAMELIZED APPLES

Making sure the skin of the belly pork is dry before you rub in the salt is the best way to ensure good crackling.

ROAST PORK WITH CRACKLING, SAGE, CIDER AND CARAMELIZED APPLES

Ingredients

1.5kg belly of pork, boned, skin on

2 cloves garlic, crushed

Handful of sage leaves, chopped

1 lemon, grated rind

2 teaspoons ground allspice plus salt and pepper

4 red eating apples, quartered, cored and sliced thickly

½ pint cider

1-2 tablespoon quince paste or marmalade

Sauce

1/2 pint cider

1-2 tablespoon quince paste or marmalade

Serves 4

1 Heat the oven to its hottest.

2 Open out the pork with the skin side down, and scatter over the garlic, sage leaves, lemon rind, allspice and seasoning. Roll up and tie. Rub salt into the skin.

3 Roast the pork for 20 minutes to crisp the crackling then turn the heat down to 140°C and cook for a further 1 ½ - 2 hours, adding the apple slices for the last 15 minutes of cooking time. Leave the pork to rest for 20 minutes before carving.

For the sauce

4 Drain off excess fat from the roasting tin and pour in the cider. Bring to the boil and add the quince paste with seasoning and continue to reduce to a good consistency.

CHOCOLATE
MERINGUE CAKE

This rich but light chocolate meringue is one of my absolute favourite puddings, and the salt adds a little mystery!

CHOCOLATE MERINGUE CAKE

Ingredients

4 egg whites

225g caster sugar

Filling

225g plain good quality chocolate

Good pinch of sea salt flakes, vanilla flavoured if possible

125ml coffee

1 pint double cream

Decoration

Flake bar or 50g (2oz) grated dark chocolate

Serves 6-8

1 Beat the egg whites till very stiff, whisk in half of the sugar bit by bit, then fold in the remainder. Spread the meringue into 3 rounds about 16cm diameter on to baking paper-lined baking sheets. Bake for 1 hour or until crisp and dry.

Filling

2 Break up the chocolate and dissolve with the salt in the coffee over gentle heat, then leave to cool.

3 Whisk the cream and add the chocolate, beating till quite stiff. Spread each meringue with the chocolate cream, layer up the cake and cover the sides with more chocolate.

4 Arrange the chocolate decoration over the entire cake.

5 Leave the cake for at least 2 hours in the fridge before serving.

SALTED OATMEAL
BISCUITS

Although they take a little time to prepare, serving your homemade savoury biscuits can make you feel quite smug!

SALTED OATMEAL BISCUITS

Ingredients

150g medium oatmeal

50g plain white flour

Pinch of bicarbonate of soda

1 tablespoon melted dripping or butter

A little boiling water

1 teaspoon sea salt flakes

1 egg white

1. Mix the oatmeal, flour and bicarbonate of soda in a bowl.

2. Pour on the melted dripping and sufficient boiling water to make a pliable dough.

3. Knead well and roll out on a floured board, very thinly into a large square.

4. Brush with beaten egg white and scatter over the salt flakes.

5. Cut into stars or triangles and bake in a moderate oven, 180°C for 15-20 minutes.

6. Serve with butter and either jam, honey or cheese.

DARK CHOCOLATE AND SALTED CARAMEL TART

Remarkably simple to make and yet this delicious tart is everyone's favourite. The layer of soft caramel in the middle is an absolute winner.

DARK CHOCOLATE AND SALTED CARAMEL TART

Ingredients

200g plain flour

2 tablespoons caster sugar

2 tablespoons cocoa powder

100g butter

2 egg yolks

½ teaspoon vanilla essence

Caramel

250g granulated sugar

125g salted butter

100ml single cream

Pinch of sea salt flakes

Chocolate Layer

2 tablespoons caster sugar

1 egg

1 egg yolk

100g plain chocolate

75g unsalted butter

Serves 6

❶ Blend all the ingredients for the pastry together and chill for ½ hour.

❷ Roll or press into a ceramic flan dish.

❸ For the caramel, dissolve the sugar in 5 tablespoons of water. Stir in the butter, bring to a bubble and then simmer for 20 minutes, stirring occasionally, until it turns light brown.

❹ Turn off the heat, stir in half the cream and when the bubbles die down, stir in the rest of the cream with the salt flakes. Cool.

❺ Press some foil around the edge of the pastry to hold it in shape then bake blind at 200°C for 12 minutes, or until it looks dry and cooked.

❻ Reduce the heat to 190°C.

❼ For the chocolate layer, whisk the sugar and eggs together until thick. Melt the chocolate and butter and beat into the eggs.

❽ Spread the caramel over the base of the tart. Spoon the chocolate mixture over the top, and bake for 12 minutes. Leave to cool and chill in the fridge.

METRIC AND IMPERIAL EQUIVALENTS

Weights	Solid
15g	½oz
25g	1oz
40g	1½oz
50g	1¾oz
75g	2¾oz
100g	3½oz
125g	4½oz
150g	5½oz
175g	6oz
200g	7oz
250g	9oz
300g	10½oz
400g	14oz
500g	1lb 2oz
1kg	2lb 4oz
1.5kg	3lb 5oz
2kg	4lb 8oz
3kg	6lb 8oz

Volume	Liquid
15ml	½ floz
30ml	1 floz
50ml	2 floz
100ml	3½ floz
125ml	4 floz
150ml	5 floz (¼ pint)
200ml	7 floz
250ml	9 floz
300ml	10 floz (½ pint)
400ml	14 floz
450ml	16 floz
500ml	18 floz
600ml	1 pint (20 floz)
1 litre	1¾ pints
1.2 litre	2 pints
1.5 litre	2¾ pints
2 litres	3½ pints
3 litres	5¼ pints

WELSH COOKBOOKS
GILLI DAVIES AND HUW JONES

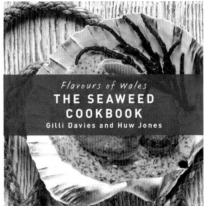

Gilli Davies does it again with three new cookbooks featuring Welsh Cakes, Seaweed and Sea Salt recipes.

Flavours of Wales Cookbooks make wonderful gifts £6.99.

Available from all good bookshops, kitchen and gift shops and online www.graffeg.com Tel 01554 824000.

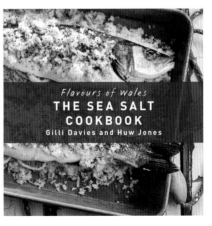

GRAFFEG

Books and Gifts from Wales

FLAVOURS OF WALES COLLECTION

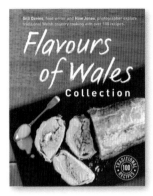

Cook up a Welsh feast with the full *Flavours of Wales* collection in cookbooks, pocket books and notecards to share with friends.

Flavours of Wales Collection book with over 100 recipes by Gilli Davies, photographed by Huw Jones £20.00

10 Recipe Notecards and envelopes in a gift pack. Full recipe inside with space for a message £8.99

Flavours of Wales Collection in a gift slip case with 5 pocke books £12.99

Flavours of Wales pocket books £2.99

Available from all good bookshops, kitchen and gift shops and online www.graffeg.com Tel 01554 824000.

GRAFFEG

Books and Gifts from Wales